A BLACK GIRL
WITH BOUNDARIES

Dedication

This book is dedicated to every girl in the world who has felt the heaviness of smothering her own feelings, wants, and desires, to please others. The girl who has had no boundaries and allowed everyone to pull her every which way except the way she needed to be pulled. The girl who can't ever stick to her own decisions, because of what looks good and what other people would have her do has always mattered more. The girl who has lost herself in her titles of daughter, sister, mom, and wife. The girl who has no voice at all.

This book is for you….girl.

~Shatara

Table of Contents

Introduction

Boundaries…. what are those???

For as long as I could remember, I was taught that you always look out for others. You put others before yourself and you definitely don't say anything to get another person in trouble (or make them be held accountable). That is what I was taught. It sounds like just a small matter, but to have that embedded in you, really makes life so difficult. You walk around on eggshells and you don't even notice it, because you want to make sure you don't hurt the feelings of others. You take loyalty to another level, because you want to show you have it, not knowing that the life you are living is not even the definition of that. You are exhausted, beyond tired, and emotionally drained and you've been that way for a while and have no idea why.

Well, I finally decided to write the book, and let you know why. You lack boundaries sis. You are not superwoman, you are not the perfect daughter, friend, sister, mom, or wife, and yet for years you have strived to be because you were taught that this is what that looks like. Working yourself to the bone, for a simple "thank you." So let me be the first to tell you: this is not how it should be! I am not sure when I found freedom in boundaries, but I have and it is more liberating than anything I have ever experienced. In this book I will outline and detail four areas where people have very little respect for boundaries and how this lack of respect has effected your adult-life: family, friends, romantic relationships, and the workplace. I am sure we all can swap stories all day of the issues we have had over the years with any of the above-mentioned entities not respecting boundaries, and even acknowledging them but still not caring.

Well, it's time out for that, it is time for EVERYBODY to respect your boundaries. I must warn you though it is not going to easy at first. You will want to give in and allow people to continue having things their way. It will be especially hard for you if you are a people pleaser or fall victim to false flattery. It will be increasingly hard for you if you develop certain attachments…. but let me slow down. I do not want to get ahead of myself. Trust me, this book is a lot to take in, and I have added note pages in between each section to journal your thoughts. Take it all in and take it easy. It is a marathon, not a sprint.

Family

Honey, I will never forget that day: I was pissed to the max! I'm over it now, but in that moment, I felt disrespected, bad, and my mama was on the other end of the phone saying, "You know it's just family stuff, that's what it is, and we have to deal with it." Ya'll I was mad and I said right then, "I don't have to deal with anything!" Oh and I was serious, and I want you to know that Mama Clark struck a nerve that day, and that was not the first time. Man, I was not trying to hear that and in retrospect, I was breaking up with the "family stuff" mentality then. I was, and that had to be almost 10 years ago now. She was basically telling me I needed to inconvenience myself for family, that I needed to be the bigger person for family, that I needed to bite my tongue for family, and all I could think was "oh heck no!" LOL!

I can laugh about it now, and I love my mama, ya'll know that, but honey she had me messed up! Needless to say, that in that season I was not where I am now, because I was obedient to her, and we moved pass it all but today I don't even think mom would ask me to do such things. Although she would probably rather me not have boundaries, she has learned to respect them. Honestly, she has boundaries too, she just does not call it that, and she get's it from my great grandmother. See here's the thing: we are so inclined to think our lives should be a revolving door for family. You know, Auntie Annie and Uncle John should be able to come and go as they please, right? People should be able to call whenever, shouldn't they?

So, my great-grandmother as the story goes secretly hated when people would pull up in the yard. Granted, back then didn't too many people have phones, so they would just pull up, but they say when my great-grandmother (you met her in Ginny's Girls) would hear and see a car outside her words were "What the hell they want?" She didn't want to be bothered, but she didn't know that it was okay to feel that way, so she opened the door and yelled, "Hey there! Come on in!" What's so funny about that is, isn't it biblical to be cheerful and show yourself friendly, so when it's fake.... never mind. You get the point.

 Mama Clark honestly inherited this characteristic. As comical and sweet as she is, she does not like to be bothered for real. She is an introvert, and an only child. She is okay with company, but it must be on her terms. Most of us are like that, we just have been programmed to not hurt anybody. I am going to break down this family dynamic the best I can though. Keep up now, and take notes:

Parents

They brought us into this world! That fact is so amazingly wonderful. In the case that your parents did not bring you into the world, but brought you up in it, that is just as wonderful. With that being said, you don't owe them for that. Let me say it again: you DON'T owe your parents for bringing you in or up in this world. They are great and believe me, I will give mine the shirt off my back, but they still must respect my boundaries. Having them respect my boundaries does not change the love I have for them. Boundaries and Love are not the same thing, and that is where we get it wrong. We think it's right or cool to say, "I'm down for my family!" "My Mama is my girl!" etc. There is nothing wrong with saying any of those things, but the problem is when you feel like you must prove it. By showing we are "down" or have unconditional love, we allow them to have their way in our adult, paying bills, lives! Believe it or not, my mom lives with me, and we can go half the day without seeing each other. She is on one end, and I am on another. We talk, and even watch movies together occasionally, but when I need silence, I have it, and when she wants to quietly watch *Gun Smoke*, she can do that.

Types of Parents

I know that not everyone has the same type of parents. Some people have really cool and laid-back parents, some have nice and pleasant parents with rules, some have extremely strict parents, and some have abusive parents be it verbally or physically. Either way, trauma is likely in most cases of upbringing and because of that trauma you must put your boundaries in place.

The Laid-Back Parent

The cool laid-back parents probably allowed you to get away with way too much. You could stay out as late you want, have visitors, go where you want, and do just about what you please. This seems really cool as a teenager, but it's not. The security blanket is not there with these parents, and they are unreliable at times. As time progresses you start to see it, how some needs were not met, how you had to fend for yourself, and how you even had to make adult decisions because you did not have a parent that could do it. This has created a problem for you when it comes to boundaries. That need to be parented and mothered is still there, so now when you have friends with that maternal instinct or older female friends, they think they can parent you because they see the need in you, but that's hard when you honestly just wanted a friend. This places a strain on the friendship and the ability to let them in without feeling like their mother hand will judge you, but here is the thing: your vulnerability gave them that opening. This is not totally your fault, but it is time that you take responsibility for the emotional damage and trauma you are carrying from your childhood so that you can establish healthy boundaries within friendships and relationships with people, leaving no room for them to believe that they can parent you. I just believe that my mom is my mom and that's that. Regardless of how she brought me up, she was charged with the task of parenting me, and whether she did it or not, it was still her duty, and I cannot lay that on anyone else, because honestly my attitude will go "who you think you talking to?" quick if it's not Barbara Clark speaking to me. LOL! In all seriousness, I say that to say we must be careful about the power we give people. Even those that mean well, may still try and that's because they have a void they are not dealing with that we have not gotten to. So, yea sis, go and deal with that so we can be healthy, happy, and whole.

The Nice, Pleasant Parents

These are the ones you owe the world, right? You could never see yourself placing boundaries on them because they have been there since birth, afforded you opportunities, supported you even when you made mistakes, showed up when it meant most and more. There is no way they need boundaries in place. Well sorry, they do. These parents also will feel like they should not have to respect boundaries. Just as they have been involved in your whole life, they believe that is permanent and should be the case throughout adulthood. So, it becomes a bit hard when dealing with these types of parents, and for lack of better words "putting them in their place." I can most certainly relate to this because I always give props to my parents for doing their very best with it came to me academically and as it relates to my extracurriculars, and I could never thank them enough for it, but I had to realize that still does not give them the right to be all up in my business and space. Now before you get all biblical on me, I understand the word of God instructs us to honor our mother and father and in no way am I encouraging anyone to dishonor them, but there is a way to tell them respectfully to respect your boundaries.

These parents mean well and just want to be involved. They want to help you pick the perfect wedding dress, give relationship advice, help with your home décor, and more. The problem is you may have your own style or way of doing things, and if you are not careful you will end up with a dress you hate, a man (who has a great job…remember, he's a good man Savannah! LOL) you are unsure about, and home décor that's just meh to you. My mom says all the time "We are so different. We don't have the same taste in clothes, food, or movies for real!" Honestly this is because I am a millennial with a baby boomer mom, but it is also because I don't allow her to force her advice on me to keep from hurting her feelings. I am honest with her. After so many years of being dishonest and trying to make her feel accomplished I realized it was not serving me. As great of a parent as she is, she does not get to dictate my decisions. Those are the things we must realize and accept. As a former educator, I appreciate nothing more than parents who are involved and intricate in their children's lives, but I also know there will come a time where that child will want to make decisions, and that parent should know to step back and support it. This is no way a level of disrespect, but a humble request to have your boundaries respected.

Sometimes it may get to a place where your parents may not understand, and they may feel offended. Prepare for that and stand your ground. You still must be respected. The thing is your parents love you and something as simple as you desiring to stand firm on your opinion or way of doing things is not the ultimate sin. If this does happen give them time to cool off and gone on about your day! They will be fine. Make sure you seal the conversation in love and keep it moving. We can't allow this little stuff to sit with us and fester. All will be well, and you all will be talking and laughing again, before you even know it. You must protect your boundaries and your peace sis. Do what is best for you.

The Extremely Strict Parents

Now these people, meant well too believe it or not. They were just too afraid of their child making a mistake that they sheltered them to the point of no return. These parents kept a strict schedule, chose the friends, the course of study, the college, the clothes, and all things involving their child. Boundaries do not exist at all in their world, and unfortunately their children are so programmed that boundaries don't exist with them either and they don't even ask for them. They never would. Their parents know best, and even if they have been out in the world a little bit, they have either ran back home, or made some big mistakes to the point that they are no longer even welcome back. The level of control they endured now makes them sometimes abuse substance, be used by others, and struggle with parenting themselves. There is a lot of potential damage that takes place when parents are too strict.

The idea though is not to protect these children from anything. It's more of a means to control. It is very sad that this happens, but it does. So how do these children get a hold on boundaries, because at this point, they allow people to come into their lives and control them, be it a husband, a friend or whoever? They have never had to stand on their own and the idea is fearful for them. They need people to run their lives like their parents did, and like I said, when they don't have people, they turn to substance. Well first, I am going to recommend therapy. At some point you need to talk to someone and get a handle the trauma that took place during your childhood. Talking and unpacking it will surely help, but you also need to follow the steps you are given to start your healing journey. From there depending on where you are in life, you would also need to prioritize. A lot of times your priorities may be mixed up in people who don't need your immediate attention, but you may need to establish boundaries with. This happens because you are searching for love and approval that you got by being obedient to your strict parents, but I can guarantee that your vulnerability is being abused and if you have children, they are being neglected.

Some of this may be hard to read especially if this is all true for you or someone you know. Now that you know that as a grown woman you do not need the approval of other grown people, you can now establish boundaries. Start saying no to things that inconvenience you, that you don't really like, and are not healthy for your household. Up until this point, anyone has been able to come into your life, and that cannot continue. Have standards and stick to them. You no longer have to prove anything to anybody.

Abusive Parents

Abuse is illegal, period. Be it verbal or physical it should never happen, but it does. Unfortunately enough, women have found themselves abused so many times at the hands of their mothers. Sad enough, mothers have a long history of being jealous of their daughters. It is like the daughter having the opportunity and a clean slate, makes the mother insane. So insane that they fail to realize they can change their lives too if they want. When this happens, boundaries become so blurred. Years of abuse at the hands of parents causes one to question every move they make, and sometimes even self-harm. It is the belief that you are not worthy of love and deserve to be treated badly. When people know this about you it breeds an endless cycle of bringing a narcissist into your life. They continue the abuse your parents started and in turn you completely allow it. You allow other people to abuse you as well and make you feel low about yourself.

Unlike the previous strict parent, this situation is a bit more intense. It is not so much that you are being taken advantage of but in this situation the abuse breaks your mental completely down, and the physical abuse can be even more harmful and sometimes result in death. If you suffered any abuse as a child, please seek help. You could very well be in an abusive situation right now and be unaware of what is truly happening because you have not set any boundaries. You don't feel that you even deserve to set boundaries. This is not true, we are all deserving, and just because your upbringing was heartbreaking it does not mean you don't individually matter. You do matter, now more than ever. Please don't let this situation get beyond your control. Stand your ground, set the boundaries, and get help.

Siblings

Sibling relationships vary so much. Literally one day they can be your best friend, the next day it is a worst enemy situation going on, and sometimes they can always be the enemy. It just depends. There are other factors too that play a role in sibling relationships, one being the age difference. When there is a huge gap in age, time periods are different, and so are views so you don't see things the same. We also must consider the wide variety of siblings you can have. There can be full mom and dad siblings, half siblings, and step siblings. For some reason though we consider mom siblings as full even if the dad is different, and I am not sure why, but we just do. It is important to remember in the back of your mind though that there are some genetic differences going on which can possibly explain a ton of things.

Now about the boundaries: the vast majority of the population would like for you to believe that whatever your siblings have going on, or take on is your problem too. I have come to tell you that this is NOT the case. I may have to type this twice, because I don't even know if it is got through the first time but let me say it a different way. Whatever your siblings have going on, does not immediately require your attention. I don't care that you are 10-15 years older and that is like your child, they are not. I don't care if you all are twins, okay you no longer share the womb. I don't care if your mom made you promise to look after each other I mean you can look out without placing yourself in situations that don't serve you. Looking out can be a phone call, text, or a cash app. That's it.

Now this may sound a bit harsh or even mean but hear me out. Children become adults and life experiences shape them. Now you and your sibling may have grown up in the same household, under the same rules and expectations, and may have even had the same mom and dad, but at some point your own personality and views begin to form, and if you had a different parent in there somehow those traits were already formed that served that genetic pull. So now as you grow older you prepare to go into the world where even more views and ideas will form. The thing is sometimes when people go in the world, they make some decisions that truly change the course of their lives, and see somehow, they want that to change the course of your life too, when it has nothing to do with you. They play the sibling card because well, you all know each other best, right? This is true, but while they want to involve you in their ill decision, they don't understand that you are dealing with your own ill decisions, you just don't call them to whine about it because your personality is you make your beds and lie in them and work at them until you can fix it! Can I get an amen somebody?

Again, this is not to be rude or anything, but I have witnessed so many people go to bat for their siblings and sacrifice time, money, and sanity for a sibling that will do the same stuff next week! They lack boundaries and they don't know how to say no cause somewhere along the way your family told you that you had to look out or your lil brother, or that your sister was a little behind, so you needed to watch her. That burden they placed on was you unfair, and you don't have to continue to do that. I can sympathize with a person having a diagnosed learning disability and you are assisting them with managing their finances and medication, but people who won't get help or help themselves, no. It is time out for that level of stress just because it is a sibling. Now before you hit me with the "brother's keeper" scripture just know, that I know my word. Listen, I am the founder and CEO of a whole non-profit that actually pays bills for women in need so I definintly am my brother's keeper, but at no time will I entertain repetitive foolishness, bring stress upon myself, or make ill decisions for the betterment of someone who could care less just to say I kept somebody. Nope.

I say all this to say, establish boundaries when it comes to siblings, no matter how closely related. We have to stop allowing people to make us feel bad when we have done nothing wrong, and by all means don't let anyone guilt trip you about your success. You worked for that, and they can work for theirs. I was guilty of this for years. I believed that whatever happened with others in my immediate family needed to be handled by me. I had to relinquish that responsibility because people are grown and grown people do what they want to do and tell you the parts they want you to know. Always keep that in mind before you throw down your boundaries and throw on your cape next time.

Auntie and Nem

This is for aunties, uncles, cousins, nieces, and nephews. Those people who are not exactly household members and you may not have ever seen them every day at any point in your life. Yep, they tend to disrespect boundaries as well. See the aunties think they know everything, and they want to be half cool with you and sometimes halfway are in competition with you when it comes to you and their children. They want to make all of these suggestions and tell you how things should go in your life, and they try to always undermine or downplay what your parents said. I remember having one particular aunt that consistently wanted my mom to allow me to spend the night with my grandma. I was never very big on staying away from home and neither was my mom big on me doing that, nor my dad. Like that was just not something we did on the regular. I think over the years she felt a certain way about my mom not just dropping me off there, but as a mom it was her job to decide where I stayed or went. That's the part where my mom established her boundary and respected mine cause well, I didn't want to go down there.

As much as we love auntie and nem, they don't run anything either. It is important to keep that in mind. The uncles, well we love them too and they always think they know best as well, but you literally have to just tune them out sometimes. They just be talking. A lot of time they have a hard time understanding us, especially if there is a generational gap. This does not mean either is wrong, it just means you have to peacefully respect the differences of opinions. This is where sometimes uncles can get a little defensive because they think they know the best financing rate, the best type of meat to buy, the best oil for your car, and so on. Learn how to gracefully bow out of these debates. I used to go toe to toe with mine (I have six of them) but over the years I realized that proving my point is not worth it all the time, and furthermore I can choose when I desire to be in their presence.

Which bring me to my next point: At no given time must you go to family functions, be it holidays or gatherings of any kind. If being there disturbs your peace, or if someone there has caused you harm physically or emotionally you do not have to go and subject yourself to them. That is literally a stronghold that has you thinking you owe it to big mama or a great aunt to still link up at her house every holiday. You don't have to do that, and it is causing you more harm than good. Family can be one of the most toxic environments, and forcing relationships there is never good. Protect your peace and love yourself better than that. Now if you are going thinking it is making the one that victimized you uncomfortable, it's not. People who have caused others pain rarely ever want to face it and are normally protected by certain family members. There is no sympathy there for you, and they honestly want you to forget it ever happened. Stop searching for something and get help, and more than anything, heal.

Now about those nieces and nephews. We love them. They are literally our babies without all of the additional things that the parents have to do. Here is one thing you must remember: they always go home with their parents. You can nurture and be "TT" all day long. You can lead, guide, and even provide but at the end of the day children in 99 cases out of 100 will choose their parents when it comes down to it. You can't take offense to it, you can't keep trying to force yourself cause that is stressing you, and these are not even your kids! Let these people have and raise their kids how they want to. The village can no longer say anything to these people about they kids. Even if you know it's a disaster waiting to happen, get in your prayer closet and war for them. That's the best you can do. The Lord will hear you, and He will make the provision. In cases like these in all seriousness you have to trust Him. People are very sensitive about their children, as they should be and when they believe they know what is right for them they will stand on that. Respect the position they have as parent but pray for what you know is the right thing. It is no different than respecting offices and positions of authority in our nation and on our jobs. Even if they are not making the right the decisions you do your part and war!

In conclusion, family is a trip ain't it? They are, but we love them, and we only want what is best for them, but not at the expense of our own sanity. My mental health matters, my life matters, my finances matter, and I can't allow anyone to place any of that in jeopardy. Do what you can and keep those boundaries in place. By all means don't take on what is not yours.

Let's Talk About It!

1. Who in your family do you NEED to establish boundaries with, and why?

____

____

____

____

____

____

____

____

____

____

____

____

____

____

____

2. Will you need therapy in your efforts to establish these boundaries
    and stick with them?

3. How soon will you work on establishing these boundaries?

Friends

Alexa, cue "What about your friends?" by TLC! I love my girls! They make life so much easier, more fun and just dope. I have friendships ranging from 2 years to 18 years, and all of them mean so much. So, the questions is: why would you need boundaries with such cool people? Well, the truth is, we need boundaries with everyone. Not anyone should be able to move how they please in our lives. It is exhausting when people can do that, and I have probably said that already, and I will probably say it again. So, let's talk about these different types of friends, and the boundaries you should have in place for them, shall we?

The Accountable Friends

These are the people who know your goals, and they are not taking your lack of not completing them. I suck at being this friend real talk. I try to hold people accountable, but I have a million things going through my brain a day and a lot of times I just forget, and if it takes a person too long to start with a goal, or they engage but get distracted, I lose interest. I have to see the action rather quickly. It does not mean I love anyone any less, I'm just human, but these friends are beyond amazing, but you better be ready for these girls. When you mess around and sleep on what you said you would do, they are coming for your head and your neck. They will not let up until it is done either. So, let's just say in the midst of you goals life starts life'n as it sometimes will. You are just not feeling it, but your girls are not letting up on it, because well although you let them in on your goals, you failed to establish your boundaries and let your very own personality show. Although they want to hold you accountable, they should also know that sometimes in the midst of getting things done you need a break mentally. They need to know that until certain goals come together in your head you can't start on them. They need to know that this does not mean you have stopped or given up, it just means you need time to work things out. When they come for you and you say "I just need time, but I got it" that should be enough for them to back off for the time being. These same friends though should know you so well should also know when it is time to come back again. I had a friend tell me that she considers the time of day, and who I am before she even calls me because she knows I am not big on phone conversation. I love that. Consider me! Again, these are the dopest friends to have, but keep in mind that your boundaries still matter. You can't just throw them all away just because you feel the pressure to succeed. The pressure is good, but your mental health and self-care matters too.

The Friend That's There When It Counts

This is the friend that shows up when it matters! They are just as dope and cool in character as the accountable friend. The thing about this friend is they have a lot going on, be it their career, family life or more, they just have a ton happening. With that being said, they can't be at every event, text back right away, or even make time to talk on the phone. You have to get with them when you can and appreciate when they do show up. This is where you have to respect their boundaries too because they can't always be there, and you have to understand that. I am sometime this friend because I can't be everywhere and when I am tired mentally, I take my breaks. I don't believe in ripping and running (whatever that means) so I take my time and plan my schedule and wherever I can't be I let the person know in advance and it's understandable. It is easy to establish boundaries with this friend by just understanding when they can't be there, and you getting that same respect from them. Also, because they can be a little aloof don't feel like you are obligated to jump when they can hang out. Work your schedule too, because it matters just as much as theirs. We are all busy sis.

The Fun Friend

Listen this girl is down for a good time, okay? She is coming with the vibes. This is the no-judgement zone friend, the shot-taking friend, the let me tell you bout my man friend! She is all about the tea and laughing until you all cry. You can get a little serious with her, but not too much, and she loves the Lord, but is not trying to get churchy in a turn-up session either. Let's just keep it cool and comfy with her, okay? In all seriousness though this friend will need to know boundaries are in place as well. There may be some areas in your life that are not a joking matter for you. You may be sensitive in these areas. You may need time to heal. For example, if your fun friend is into talking about sex, and you are practicing abstinence, it may not be easy for you to hear those things. If you are on a fast, heading to a bar with the fun friend may not be smart. In turn they have to be understanding, because that is who you are and those are the boundaries you have in place. The fun friend is adventurous so there may even be places you can't venture off to with them. Always keep the fun friend near because she is a sweetheart. Be there for her because she is surely going to be there for you.

The Friend That Needs You

I did my best not to call her the needy friend, but you get my point. She is not necessarily needy, but she requires a bit more TLC than others. Here is the thing, you have to be very clear about what you will do and what you won't do when it comes to them and never bend the rules. We are not in the business of tricking people, so don't ever let people think they stand on a non-existent pedestal. You have to make it very clear what you will not do with this friend. The moment you start getting out of your bed at night assist them in "situations," the moment you start answering your phone for them at work or in places you should not, the moment you start being at their beck and call they will confuse your commitment to this friendship and believe boundaries are non-existent, and that is unhealthy for you. Now if you suffer from the "need to be needed" syndrome you may be okay with this little arrangement, but that is still unhealthy. Needing to be needed makes you fall victim to false flattery. You know those people who say, "Girl you have to be there, it just won't be the same without you!" Why it won't? Like for real what does your absence change when it comes to something they can do with or without you? People love to do that because they think you need that, and those that need to be needed do need that. You cannot run yourself, your mind, your body, and your vehicle down trying to be everywhere for everybody. If you can help it sit down sometimes. You don't always have to be on the road, and honestly that's how so much goes wrong. So be mindful when people say they "need" you. You need you too.

In conclusion, you may have friends that are a combination of any of these, and that's cool too. No matter where they stand, they are all dope to have around, but you have to make sure that you take care of your mental and establish your boundaries so that you don't get overwhelmed when it comes to them. They are amazing, and you want these relationships for years to come. Don't let the lack of boundaries ruin it, because sometimes when you are running yourself crazy trying to maintain a friendship you get so drained from not having boundaries, and then you end things on a tough note, when really having boundaries could have changed all of that. Keep your life balanced and peaceful with boundaries.

Let's Talk about It

1. So, which of the above listed friend types are your favorite, and
    who is your friend that fits into it? Express your thoughts about her.

____

____

____

____

____

____

____

____

____

____

____

____

____

____

____

____

____

____

2. Now that you understand how to put boundaries in place when it comes to friends, how do you think it will go for you and your friendships?

____

____

____

____

____

____

____

____

____

____

____

____

____

____

____

____

3. Do you have a relief now that you understand what has been probably stressing you for so long when it comes to friendships?

Relationships.... The Romantic Kind

Prepare to be sick of me, cause when the time comes all you will hear is….."my man, my man, my man!" Just kidding! For real though, as unlucky in love as I have been, I still believe in love, God's design for marriage, and all of that. I just believe when the Lord's will is involved people can have their hearts desire and that includes a successful marriage. So, I know we all know about being equally yoked, leaving and cleaving, and all of that right? Good, well there still have to be boundaries in place, even when it comes to relationships. I am not going to confuse relationships with marriage here because it is important to note there is a difference, a huge one. When it comes to boundaries, I am going to respect the sanctity of marriage and only address boundaries in relationships. I am an unmarried woman; therefore, I understand that there are certain lines that I should not cross. So, let's talk about it, shall we?

New Love

Okay so this may not even be love because it's so new, but isn't it awesome to meet someone you can vibe with, that seems to possibly be the one? Like there is nothing like newness. You want to spend time with them as much as possible, you text and talk on the phone until you fall asleep, everything is just perfect. Because it has been so long since you felt a love like this, you go all in with no boundaries in sight. You just want to make this man happy and enjoy his amazing company. This is a mistake, and a commonly made one that is just easy to make, because when you are happy you just let your guard down. Don't let insecurities and fear of being alone make you give up everything for anyone. Granted I am beyond ready to let my guard down, but I will not be letting my boundaries go. I want to be fancy free and sleep just as peaceful as I am now, but still have this man respect my tight schedule, boundaries, and necessary flexibility. Rearranging your life cannot happen just because you have met a nice guy. You should be happy with yourself, first just for giving love a chance, but you cannot just drop everything or anything because he's in your life. This is new, so at this point you need to compartmentalize him, not prioritize him. If he is pursuing you properly he will understand. Trust me that no matter how tight your schedule is, grown people make time for what they want. Men have been doing this for years. They will not skip the gym, they frat, or the Superbowl party for you, no matter how cute you are. This is new, and he does not know if this is going to go anywhere, and you don't know either so just because it's good, don't force it. Make it clear what you have time for and go from there. One thing about me, I hate talking on the phone and would rather do short face times and text. I hope God sends a man that's down for that cause I just can't be talking on no phone.

Long-Term Relationship

Alright now! You all have graduated to a real, real relationship. How sweet? This is amazing, and it is my prayer that marriage is the goal and where you are going. As this relationship progresses of course you have started to make more time for your significant other, because he has become significant in your life, but the key is knowing the correct timing in doing that. Lucky for you, if you followed the steps above you set your relationship up so that you would not have to let go of everything to maintain it. Because you know that your life matters too, and your boundaries should be in place, I can guarantee that this is an amazing relationship. I always said that relationships don't call for separate lives, but they do call for individuality. When individuals can bring themselves to the table, and support each other, something beautiful can be created. Although I will not go into detail about marriage, I do know that setting up these boundaries now, will keep those things in mind when marriage is on the table. I remember having a guy tell me once, that he did like me, and wanted me, but he did not think he could handle all there was to me. There were so many things he took issue with that I knew he was not the one, although a part of me tried to force it, I knew I could not do that to myself. *TyTalks* was just taking off at this time, and writing a book was not even on the radar. So, imagine had I hid myself and continued that relationship in hopes of marriage? You would not be reading this book, that is for sure.

With all of that being said as it pertains to relationships and boundaries, be careful. Relationships give you the butterflies and it just always feels good to be loved and loved on. You are placed in positions to have to care about the feelings of another, and to make them feel better when they aren't. This is quite the role, and a beautiful one to say the least. It is my hope though that the role does not consume you and you are able to still hold on to you own dreams, businesses, brands, and all that you have to offer the world.

Let's Talk About It!

1. Are you currently dating someone? Have you been able to still work towards your goals in this relationship? Why or why not?

2. What are your thoughts on marriage and children? Be 100% honest
    and unapologetic here.

____

____

____

____

____

____

____

____

____

____

____

____

____

____

____

____

____

____

3. Do you feel secure enough to establish your boundaries and stick with them when you do enter a relationship?

The Work Place

There literally came a time when my co-workers and I were motivated to come to work simply because we got to laugh with each other. Granted we loved our job, and we loved those kids, but life had become hard and rigid, and the fun was taken out of education. It honestly hurt to feel that way but at least we had each other. I am sure some people have bonds with their co-workers like this, but I know there are plenty who don't have that. Either way, the workplace needs boundaries, and you should not be bound by your workplace. There are three areas within the workplace where you need to practice boundaries: with your superiors, colleagues, and those you serve.

Superiors

These are the people that sometimes praise you for your efforts, and other times make you feel that you are not good enough. It is so hard sometimes to know where you stand with them. Sometimes they are moody, and other times they are pretty cool to be around. You can't ever let your guard down with them and must always be on your p's and q's even if you are just appearing to be. Although all of this is true, don't get it twisted, there is still a thing called Human Resources that handles all paperwork pertaining to you, and that should always be your biggest concern: salary, hours, personal leave, sick leave, and vacation leave, those are the things that matter the most and they control how you process what your superiors desire believe it or not. A lot of leaders don't understand that it is truly how you treat your staff that constitutes their behavior. When people are treated well, they are happier about serving. Some leaders like to believe that a nice check and retirement is enough to keep people around and that should make them serve but it doesn't. Their honest days' work, earned that. You cannot put a price on kindness. Now when it comes to your focus (HR), utilize your leave, as much as you like and your insurance. Don't ever let your superiors make you feel bad about taking off. That is your time, and that job will be there when you return, trust me. I always tell people to never be upset about how fast a job replaces an employee after death, be upset that they did not choose themselves in life and utilize their leave. Establish those boundaries and put yourself first, and don't ever get it twisted that, that job "needs" you, and things won't go well if you are not present; they will figure it out. Again, thinking like that is falling victim to false flattery. I am not a fan of that if you haven't been able to tell. Being flattered by people triggers the concept of the slave mentality for me. If I am going too deep forgive me, but it does. It is okay to be loved, but just don't let people manipulate you. That's all. Set your boundaries, take your leave, make your appointments, and live your life.

Colleagues

These can be your best friends, fake friends, or enemies. It is up to you if you care or not. So many time people say, "I didn't come here to make friends" and honestly, I find that kind of rude to say out loud. Mind you I am a people person, so I see nothing wrong with making friends on the job. If you show yourself friendly, what do you expect happen, and if you don't show yourself friendly people will think you are a......you know. The whole "no new friends" concept is just immature because as you progress thorough this life, you will most certainly meet some great people, and don't let anyone make you feel that you can't befriend them. If you meet colleagues that show themselves friendly give friendship a try, with boundaries of course. You can be their friends, but always be honest with them when it comes to the job as well. If your goal is advancement, make that clear, and use your boundaries to ensure that they understand that this does not mean you are going to change, you just have goals. Be sure to not allow them to change your mind about your goals as well. There is a line between being their friend and wanting more. I remember applying for a higher position and having colleagues as friends. I let them know. I did not want to walk into an interview that they were in and hadn't told them. It just didn't sit right with me. So don't be afraid to be friends with your colleagues. Mature people can handle this relationship, and if you run from it, you may cheating yourself out of some really dope people.

The People You Serve

In most careers, there is a duty to a group of people you serve. A lot of times they will request things beyond your scope of assistance, and they know it is beyond it, but they ask anyway. Keep your boundaries intact, most jobs won't even allow certain favors, and on top of that you just don't want to be the one giving out freebies, and other things that you should not, and people get greedy. You can do something one time for someone, and they will believe that you always owe them that favor and keep coming back for more with no care about how it may affect you. This boundary is honestly just wisdom, and as much as we like to help people when we have the power to do so, we just can't. Your job is trusting you, and you should not betray that to appear as anything in front of the people you serve, even if they become upset. Always remember that rules are rules, and right is right and people who don't live by that rarely make it far in life. You will always have to follow protocols in life and having people respect your boundaries is making them follow your protocols.

Let's Talk About It

1. Do you feel guilty about taking days off from work? Why or why not?

____

____

____

____

____

____

____

____

____

____

____

____

____

____

____

____

2. Have you ever felt guilt about leaving a job or being promoted at a job? If so, how did you deal with it with your colleagues?

3. How do you handle people asking your favors as it pertains to your job? If you haven't been handling it, how will you handle it in the future?

Listen, I truly enjoyed writing this for my black girls with boundaries, but honestly, I wrote for all girls, because we all need to establish those boundaries. I know it's not easy telling the people you love they can't always have access to you, your possessions, or any and everything connected to you, but you have to. You will never have anything if you allow people to come into your life and keep taking at their whim. It is really not fair to you, and I challenge you to stand up for yourself, this day. If ever you are torn, you can always open this book again, and start over. The lessons here will never get old, and if people truly love you, they are not going anywhere. Now they get mad for a little bit, but that's okay. Stand your ground, keep your boundaries in place, and let your peace unfold!

Love ya girl!

About the Author

A native of Cuba, Alabama, Miss Shatara S. Clark, is a proud alumna of Alabama A&M University, and Auburn University at Montgomery. Shatara strongly believes in the educating of young people, as she taught in secondary education for 10 years. Currently she is employed as a Grant Evaluator for organizations and companies. Her absolute joy is assisting others.

Aside from her career, Shatara also free lances as a writer, blogger, author, and self-publisher. Shatara strives to assist her clients and offer them a stress-free experience. She is also the founder of a non-profit 501c3 organization, *TyTalks*, which has a mission to empower women across the globe to embrace who God has called them to be doing this by offering free or low-cost conferences, workshops, seminars, and more. Shatara loves to serve her community. She is a proud member of Delta Sigma Theta Sorority Incorporated.

Currently Shatara is on a book tour titled **Better Together** where she and a partner on tour feature a different author at each stop. The goal is to promote other authors and give them opportunity to showcase their work. Aside from the book tour, **Better Together** has also established the **Distinguished Authors of Alabama Award**. This award is given to those that meet certain requirements and are given the honor after an application and interview process. When Shatara is not busy with her many ventures, she enjoys traveling, dining, writing, and resting.

For More Information Visit

Facebook: Shatara S. Clark

Instagram: mstytalks

Email: info@allthingstywrites.com

www.allthingstywrites.com